Friends with Lights
A True Story

by

Psychic Medium & Healing Energy Channel

Judi Lynch

Copyright © 2011 Judi Lynch

All rights reserved.

ISBN-13: 978-0615580081 (Judi Lynch)
ISBN-10: 0615580084

DEDICATION

This book is dedicated to every soul who thought they were lost until they found a friend with a light. And to my baby girlfriend Anni Lu, sweetest dog I ever knew. Rest in beautiful peace, sweet girl.

We are beings of Shining Light, Loved Unconditionally.

CONTENTS

	Acknowledgments	i
1	Visiting Souls	3
2	Life Changing Events	6
3	Shining Lights	8
4	Awakening the Energy	11
5	The Crystal and the Spirit Guide	14
6	Where are You?	17
7	A Friend with a Light	18
8	Message for my Neighbor	25
9	The First Healing	28
10	Soul Messages and Visits	30
11	Sharing the Light	34

ACKNOWLEDGMENTS

Thanks to God and everyone who has been a part of the journey.
Special thanks to Linda C. Owen, Dr. Louise Mallory-Elliott, Char, Kim, Jack,
Mike, JV, Scott, Linda, Liz & Mike, Kumi, Derrick, Anni & Tinki, Chris &
Liane. Thanks for everything and all you are, Judi

1 VISITING SOULS

My earliest memory of life on Earth began when I was four years old. It was my 4th Birthday party. I remember a huge bright light setting me down at a picnic table in our backyard. In a matter of seconds, I was opening my presents. One of those presents was a little stuffed cat made with rabbit fur. It looked real! I said, "Whose bright idea was this! I'm not allowed to have a cat!" and everyone laughed. I have no memory of things before that and I told friends all through my childhood about that light. I didn't know what it was or what it meant but I could never forget it. I was so bright yet it didn't hurt my eyes and I remember looking up and thinking I had just arrived from somewhere else. Where, I didn't know.

When I was five I had no idea what was going on in my world that other people couldn't see. I told my Grandma Lucy that her husband was sitting on the couch next to her one day. She said I sure was mean because I knew he had been dead for many years. I said I knew that he was, but he was still sitting right there! I told my mom that Grandma sure needed some new glasses! We made friends later when she showed me how to play solitaire and blackjack and I told her I'd be quiet about it if I saw anyone else sitting there and playing cards with us that she couldn't see.

I also remember falling asleep during nap time once at school and seeing my friend Denise fall down and scrape her knee out on the playground during her class recess. I woke up wondering if she was okay. After school she showed me her injury. I didn't know then what astral travel was. I only knew I had wanted to be outside on the playground all the time so I guess I must have traveled there whenever I got the chance.

When I was nine, my friend's mother was killed in a train accident just a couple of blocks from our back door. I was sitting in my room when her mother came to me and told me to please tell everyone that she was okay, she was in Heaven. She wanted her kids to know she would always send help to watch over them. I ran down the street and told my friend that her mom wasn't dead. I said I had just seen and talked to her at our house! She was floating in the air in a big light! She ran down to our house to see and told my mom what I had said. My mother slapped me across the face and I cried all night long. My eyes were so swollen that I could hardly see the next day. I knew she had been there but no one believed me. I thought I was doing something good to help my friend. I was too young to understand why I had gotten in so much trouble. A short time later my little friend took a hammer and broke apart a huge amethyst crystal that belonged to her Dad and gave me a big piece. She said I should have it but she didn't know why. It's sitting on my dresser all these years later after always being in my jewelry box. I never forgot where it came from. It was special to me for many reasons, some I didn't know until later.

I spent the first few years of my childhood attending a Southern Baptist Church every week. They told us we were all sinners and if we didn't obey the words in the Bible, we were all going to Hell. I questioned everything. I was told to be quiet and listen and obey. The Summer I turned eleven, I went to Baptist camp in rural Indiana. One afternoon while I was out enjoying the day's activities, one of the camp counselors broke into my suitcase. She took a seam ripper and ripped the seams out of all my new dresses, saying they were too short. I never went back to the Baptist church again. I wasn't about to follow all their silly rules. I had a faith that no one could shake and none of these people could answer my questions or explain how I knew things or saw things they couldn't see. When I was 12, I joined a Methodist church because they had a youth group and we could wear whatever we wanted.

Though I had asked for the visiting souls to go away, I still had a few more encounters that I explained away as dreams. One of those visits occurred in High School when I was 16. I woke up one morning knowing what had happened to my friend's boyfriend the night before. He had been in a horrible car accident on his way home from a family get-together and he came to me and told me how much he cared about her and to please make sure she knew. That morning I woke up and called her house immediately and she told me that his sister had just called her to let her know. She asked me how I knew about it. Why would his sister call me? It was 7 AM. I was confused and didn't know exactly what to say. I told her that his sister must have called when I was half asleep. I knew everything that had happened in the accident and I told her I was coming over. In this crazy dream I thought I'd had, he had begged me to go and see if she was all right. She insisted that her mother was there and she would get through this. She said I really didn't have to come over. I still felt this overwhelming need to comfort her even though I didn't understand it. I went to her house later that morning and I knew without a doubt that the information I had received wasn't a dream. I know that I woke up in the middle of the night and he was there and he told me about the accident and about his feelings for my friend. He was just a teenager, we thought he had a whole life in front of him, and he was gone in an instant.

Later that year another friend died violently in a home invasion. He also visited me one night and told me that he had been getting up his nerve to finally ask me out on a date and suddenly he was in the wrong place at the wrong time. He told me it had seemed so unreal when it happened. Again, I thought his visit had just been a dream of wishful thinking, but a girl I knew told me the very same thing at his funeral. She walked up to me and said "Did you know that he had a crush on you but was too shy to say anything?" Yeah, I knew but I didn't tell her how he had told me.

Not too long after that, I woke up in the middle of the night thinking that another friend's boyfriend had somehow gotten in my bedroom. He was standing at the end of my bed telling me that he needed my help. I said you are not supposed to be in my room and how did you get in here! He said I think I'm in trouble and I need to know where to go. I told him to go home and he said that he tried no one could see him there. He told me he had walked right through everyone! I said "Oh No! That means you're supposed to go to heaven then." He told me that was all he needed to know and thanked me for my help. I went back to sleep and once again probably thinking, what wonderful ridiculous dreams I have! The next afternoon someone called to tell me that he had been killed in a motorcycle accident. I told them that I already knew but I didn't know who had called me, I must have been asleep. Again, I didn't know what else to say.

My first real job at 16 was working in the basement of a cemetery as a telemarketer. We had to call people every evening after dinner and ask them if they had a burial plot for the big day. A great job for a psychic teenager! I used to try and scare everyone by telling them there was a ghost on the stairs or something in the closet. We had some frightening times in a few night thunderstorms when the power went out.

BOOK TITLE

2 LIFE CHANGING EVENTS

I have lived my life gathering experiences and friends and knowledge. I always knew I had certain "psychic things" going on but it wasn't something I had time to focus on. I also had lots of experience and love for music and entertainment. As a child and young adult, I took classes in dance, guitar, piano, music theory and performed in choirs for several years. As an adult I started writing and recording my own music. I performed with several bands and had the amazing experience of recording in some of the best studios in Nashville and working with many gifted and famous musicians and producers. I have to be completely honest and admit that I was deeply disappointed by the treatment of women in the industry. I didn't stop writing but I was disillusioned. My dream of writing songs for established artists was left behind even though I had signed several song contracts, I stopped going to songwriters nights and I stopped recording. I bought a computer and taught myself how to do graphic design.

In the early 90's, I had left NW Indiana for Alabama. There was so much negative energy and rage near the city (Chicago) and surrounding areas that I felt extremely anxious. Several people I knew had recently been murdered and the tone was dangerous. A friend's daughter and my lawyer were both murdered. One morning our neighbor was killed by a bomb wired to his truck ignition. There were problems with gangs and our neighborhood was rapidly changing. I grew very anxious and concerned. Even going out alone to the grocery store or the mall was a stressful ordeal. I felt such a strong pull to move away from there and to change our lives and live somewhere not quite so angry and violent. Everything there felt so gray to me. Yes, gray is the word for it. I couldn't see any light there anymore at all. A big part of me knew I had to get closer to the Earth and breathe in the air to heal from all the stress and trauma.

One very profound psychic experience happened in Indiana before my family and I moved. My husband and I were riding in the back of a friend's car on our way to play carpet golf with him and his wife. I had an acute anxiety attack while we were driving. I told my husband to never ever get in the car with this friend again! Even though I didn't know where or when, there was going to be a life changing accident. I had heard a loud boom and twisting metal and it haunted my thoughts everyday. We continued to go places and spend time with them, but we always drove ourselves to the activities from then on. He warned his friend about my "premonition" but they laughed it off saying it was because he drove too fast and made me nervous. I knew it was more than that. A few months later this friend invited my husband to go to Chicago for a Bears game. Free tickets and the Bears! I knew he wanted to go but I begged him to please politely decline the tickets unless he was going to drive. He remembered my warning and politely declined the invite and said we had other plans.

Early that Sunday morning, we received a phone call from our friend's wife. He had been killed on his way to pick up the Bears tickets from his parent's home. His car was hit and completely demolished by a fast moving train. The warning signals had not been installed yet and were lying in the grass by the tracks. If my husband had said yes to the trip, he would have been in that car. He lost one of his best friends that day and he told me he would never doubt my ability to "know" things again.

3 SHINING LIGHTS

We needed a quieter life; we sold the house, quit our jobs, packed up everything and moved. I felt I was on my way to changing my life by slowing down and opening up my heart and my mind and discovering a whole different way of thinking. I was turning down the noise. I also had a very real warning that my father's health was going to worsen. He had taken early retirement and he and most of the rest of my family were in Alabama now.

Two years after I moved, my paternal Grandmother died after complications from pneumonia and the flu after a car accident. A few months later, my Father died from cancer. One morning I woke up and my Grandmother was standing in my room near the dresser. Then she faded out and was gone. I missed them both dearly. My house was between where both of them had lived.

It was because of my grief that I started reading about things I had never read about before. I found a book called *Adventures of a Psychic* about Sylvia Browne. This woman claimed that she could get messages from those on the other side. I loved her personality, she made me laugh. She also gave me comfort and hope. I also agreed with the spiritual information she was sharing and it made so much sense to the way I also believed things to be.

One morning I woke up, jumped out of bed and ran to the window. I saw a huge silent light shining down on the lawn. So bright, but it didn't hurt my eyes! So calming, so warm, it felt like a big hug of love. The light I had seen as a child was back and it looked like it was parked over my house. It looked like a helicopter was hovering over and shining a spotlight down on me. I might have thought it was a helicopter if it hadn't been completely silent. This was a sign to me that I was finding that Light I had long ago forgotten was available to me. I was wide awake and I know what I saw.

One day a friend at work handed me a book and said it changed her life. I could hardly put it down. Why did all of this sound so familiar? Could all of this really be possible? Why does it make so much sense to me? That book was the *Celestine Prophecy* by James Redfield. So thank you Linda C. Owen wherever you are now! When I met you, you were a graphic designer who wanted to study energy healing. You gave me this book and you moved to Utah and I never saw you again. You are one of the people who helped me to change my life and find a deeper purpose.

I finished that book and thought about all these new concepts I wanted to explore. I went to the used book store just down the highway and looked for anything they might have about psychic communication. I wanted to know more about how I could communicate again. The only book they had on the shelf about this was *We Don't Die, George Anderson's Conversations with the Other Side* by Joel Martin and Patricia Romanowski. On the back of the book it said: "This is a book that will open your mind to an infinite realm of possibility, reassurance, and spiritual growth." It was so true!

I was truly fascinated with the people who were communicating. I wanted to understand and know more. I read more books by these authors and several others to keep these concepts flowing in my mind. I didn't know too many people personally that I could discuss this with. These books also truly made me understand that I had to get myself back on track and find my spiritual self. And for the next several years, I worked on trying to be the person that I needed to be inside. I read, I experienced, I wrote and I went out and lived a life. I sought ought new adventures and made new friends. I worked on myself because I knew I had let myself get gray and careless.

I had felt so overwhelmed with all the things I could not control around me. I started applying the concepts I learned to my life and everything started to change for the better. I knew I had life themes to complete or overcome and I learned better how to deal with other people who didn't understand me. I worked on keeping my energy positive and removing myself from as much negativity as possible.

During 2005 I had been going through a lot of changes in my life. I had quit my graphic design job working on a NASA contract for a big company contractor. For several reasons (the major one being the constant neck pain and migraines), I decided I wanted to have a career where I could work at home. So I studied interior decorating and design with a couple of online and correspondence courses and started a small business. My pain was still there but at least I could make my own hours and set my own goals.

I also started spending more time on my spiritual studies and writing down goals. I joined an online community to gain more knowledge. I reread books that rang true to my psychic soul. I had time to think about my life and I also knew that my neck pain was getting worse and my migraines were more severe. Throughout the years, I had been to several doctors about the curvature in my neck and the disc problems and the bone spurs, etc. The last doctor (a neurologist) told me I could never live with this pain, and that I would have to have surgery sooner or later. I opted for never. The problems were too close to my spine and I knew there was no guarantee I would ever be out of pain or if what they wanted to do would require a lifetime of more surgeries or procedures. I knew that there was something else out there coming along to help me, but I didn't know what it was yet. During this time I adopted a little Jack Russell terrier mix named Anni, and her sweet personality helped me when I was in a lot of pain. She channels great energy and unconditional love.

I pressed on with my little business but spending a lot of time hurting and recovering. I got very depressed but it was just what I needed to wake up and listen to what my body was telling me. It was time to heal. Time to heal everything! I was ready. I kept praying, listening, meditating, reading and discovering. I asked for my spiritual gifts to be made stronger and the Universe set up a chain reaction of events to make it happen. It might be a cliché', but you really better be ready for what you ask for!

4 AWAKENING THE ENERGY

At the suggestion of several people in an online spiritual discussion group, I made plans to attend the Galactic Expo in Nashville in the spring of 2006. I had no idea I was going to feel the rush of soul energies and float away on a cloud that day, but I did.

They had suggested a couple of people for me to stop by and talk to or have a reading with and I sought out those people. The first one was a psychic named Sean who told me several interesting things about myself along with this "You have many gifts, and more are coming to you which you will learn how to use." He was very intuitive and informative and he gave me a marvelous confidence that I was supposed to be there that day.

One of my most important objectives at the New Age Expo was in finding Dr. Mallory Elliott. I was told I should really try to meet and talk with her or attend her seminar there at the expo. I walked up to her booth and told her my friends had recommended I see her while I was there. She didn't ask my name and asked me to sit down in one of two chairs. I sat down and she stood behind me. I could feel the heat and the energy even though I could not see her and she never physically touched me. I felt energy above my head and behind me. I closed my eyes and she started the meditation. She told me she was taking me on a light journey to the other side. Pretty soon it felt as if we were floating and I could feel white light pouring in through the top of my head. I felt so light and so free, it was a feeling of peace and happiness that I had remembered feeling what seemed like an eternity ago. All the negativity was melting away. It was awesome and glorious, taking away all my fears and doubts about anything. Angels, lots of them, standing in that same light I had seen before. So bright, but soft at the same time, you can look right into it. There are no more words I can think to write to describe it…

When we came back to the reality of the booth in the middle of the expo building, she picked up the other chair and moved it closer to mine, sitting right next to me. She almost whispered in my ear, "There is no other way to put this to you, because we don't believe in hiding the truth and you have found your way to me now. You are incredibly gifted psychically with more to come if you want and ask for it to. You are someone who already has the power to ask for anything you want, just ask. Surround yourself with light consciousness. The connection is already there. I'm sure you already know this."

I was still stuck to the chair in awe. I know what I saw, I know what I felt. It validated all these wild and crazy things that had been happening all my life. All the warnings, visits from spirits, white lights and synchronicity, made more sense now. Everything that has happened to me that led me to this place right here today. There were two people waiting in line to speak with her, so I told her I would be back later in the afternoon with a question or two. I walked back to her booth a couple of hours later and asked for her advice. Should I take classes? What could I do with these "gifts"? She told me her visions. She said "You certainly don't need my help to communicate with spirit; you do it all the time." "You are going to find you own way to communicate with spirit and use these gifts, you can pretty much ask for anything, it's up to you to decide." She asked me if I thought it was my purpose to be a healer. She asked me how I wanted to be able to talk to spirit, that I could decide and that all I really needed was confidence it could be done. I asked her if she could explain to me how I could communicate directly (see, hear out loud) and she said I had my own way of doing things, and it would become more clear to me. I thanked her with all my heart and floated off into the afternoon.

I may have forgotten how to see them, but I could feel them everywhere at that expo, all around me. There were souls gathered there from all over, they were even making the curtains swish back and forth. It was the happiest I had felt in a long time and physically I was in relief. It was absolutely awesome! My pain was diminished and leaving me, and I felt like I was actually walking on air.

April 2006 Dr. Mallory-Elliott (on the left), and me (on the right).

5 THE CRYSTAL AND THE SPIRIT GUIDE

When I returned home in Alabama, I was frantic to find a clear crystal pendulum that someone had given me a couple of years before. I used to have it hanging in a window and had never gotten around to putting it up again. I found it in a drawer. I wanted to feel that energy coming through. I had to know if I could really start communicating the way I wanted to so badly. I had so many friends and loved ones that I missed. Could they find me? I knew from all my studies and experiences that we were all supposed to have a Spirit Guide around us. I wanted this guide to validate their presence and their identity. I kept asking questions holding the pendulum steady between my fingers and watching the energy give me the answers. Back and forth for yes and round in a circle for no. It never changed always gave me that formula and all the answers were strong and made sense.

I also started listening to the Ascension meditation CD by Dr. Louise Mallory-Elliott every single night before bed. Dr. Mallory-Elliott is the same woman who gave me the five minute session back at the expo and opened up what I now know is my crown chakra. She helped me to let the light back in. Thank God for wonderful souls like Louise! An online spiritual friend named Char had sent me the CD months before, but it wasn't until I met Louise in person, that I realized how special these meditations were!

I worked on this day and night and the energy grew stronger and stronger and pretty soon I needed to be able to grow beyond yes and no using the crystal. I needed to know who was out there. I needed more validation. It was at the point that I knew I had messages coming through that I could not hear and I had to know what they were. I didn't want to just "know" things anymore. I had to feel it and see it again   I asked for it and prayed for it to be.

With extreme determination, I got a piece of paper and wrote the alphabet one morning. I took the pendulum and I moved it over the letters to see if the energy would pull to spell out anything. I wanted anything that would tell me something in more detail. I knew my guide was here, but I wanted a name. I wanted information and more communication. No way was I going to let this go. I could physically feel the energy growing around me. I also learned very quickly that you had better remember to say your prayers and light those white candles because a couple of ghosts almost scared me half to death. Although they couldn't harm me, I wasn't ready for the answers to the questions that I asked one of them.

The first time I held that crystal pendulum over that letter chart, I could not comprehend what was happening. It started pulling from letter to letter spelling out words. I sat there staring down at the table for what seemed like several minutes, wondering if I had imagined it. Was I just really tired or was I now getting letters and words. This energy was talking to me. But who was I talking to?

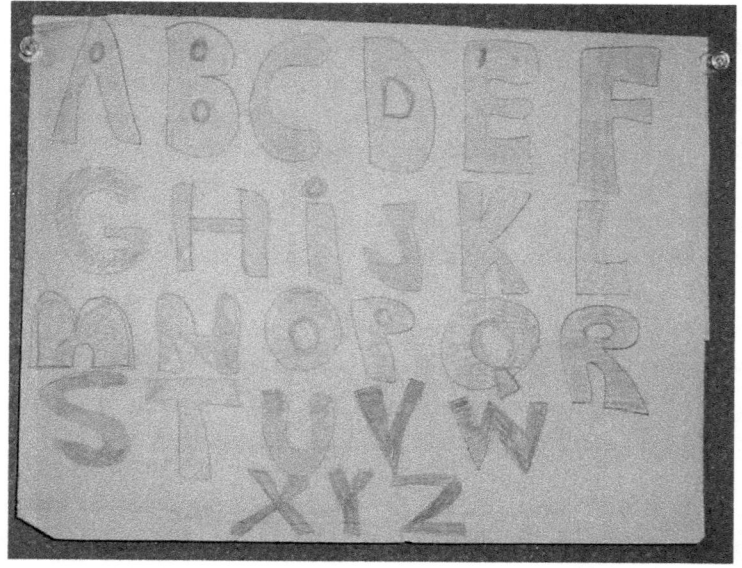

I started asking questions and I started getting answers. The first word spelled out to me was "Jack" I asked if he was my Spirit Guide. The answer was yes. I asked who else was there. The answer was "Emma" Emma's energy was very different somehow and I asked her who she was. Her answer on the letter chart was "ghost". I jumped up from the table! I had not expected that! I put everything away, and went to bed.

The next morning (after tossing and turning all night) I tried again. This time I lit a candle, I said a prayer and I asked Jack not to bring anymore ghosts around. I wasn't ready for it. I asked to talk to him and he started talking. It took hours and hours to work this way. He was channeling words and sentences through the crystal in my right hand over a letter chart while I wrote them down with my left hand. He answered questions and gave me advice. One of the first things he told me was to read Dyer. I thought he must be talking about Wayne Dyer and when I asked, the answer was yes. Jack told me about the life he had lived on Earth before agreeing to become my spirit guide and a whole lot more.

I got brave enough one day and asked about several of my friends and loved ones. I inquired about an old caving and hiking buddy (and good friend) of mine who had crossed over in 2001. And the next thing I knew, he was there. We channeled several messages and then…

I asked him about another friend who had been in a car accident the year before. Had he seen him there on the other side? His answer was no. I asked Jack if my friend was there in Heaven. His answer was no. I knew something was wrong. If he wasn't there, where else would he be? Were they not getting through correctly? What was it that I didn't understand? There was no doubting this incredible energy and all the other communication I was getting. So I guess I had to find him then. I had to know.

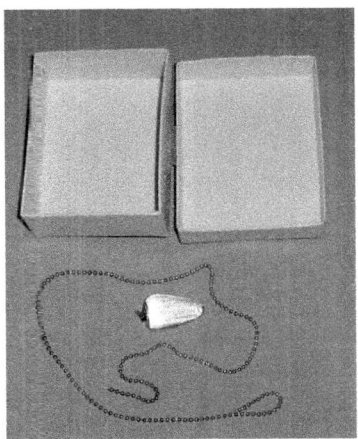

6 WHERE ARE YOU?

Determined to find out what was going on, I sat down the next morning and asked my friend if he was here, was he around me? The energy running through my pendulum answered yes. I asked him if he was all right, and he answered no. My first instinct was to think that he was still just a little mad about the way he had died so young and he wanted to express it. But the more the messages came through, it became clear that he was not where he was supposed to be and I didn't understand why.

If I could communicate with him and he wasn't on the Other Side, then that could only have meant that he had stayed here. And if he had stayed here then how did he find me and how was he communicating with me if he was a ghost, since I had asked for a hold on that please!

He was in was in complete spiritual panic but at the same time we could not believe we were talking to each other. Of course the reason we could communicate is because I spoke to him and his energy came through... and he had been looking for someone to help him. He had heard me say his name! "Mike, are you there?"

I stayed confused for awhile but I kept asking questions and then I realized that he was afraid to cross over. I could not believe that this had really happened to him. He said he did not understand what was in that Light and he wasn't going. He asked me what would happen to him when he got there. He wanted to know what kind of trouble he was in and was afraid they wouldn't even let him in. I asked him what was happening to him now where he was. And I was sorry I asked!

He said that he was being chased by mean souls where he was and that he had not lived his life like he should have. He was afraid of being judged. He said he had checked on his family and friends after the accident and they had suspected him of drinking and driving that evening (which he had not done). He said he had become so upset by this he had stayed around to try to make them hear or see him somehow, but he soon realized that they couldn't. No one could hear him, no one could see him. Until I picked up that crystal and he heard me say his name through the consciousness...

7 A FRIEND WITH A LIGHT

Once I realized what was going on, I asked him if he could see a light where he was. He said a yes, a little bit, that he could see a little bit of a bright light. Then he asked me if I could see him sitting on a box in front of the table I was sitting at. I said no. I know you're here, your words are getting through but I cannot see you with my eyes. His words were being channeled through the crystal the same way my guides were and his energy was frantic and panicked. He kept asking me if I could see him and his energy kept moving around the room. He wouldn't cross over and he didn't want me to stop channeling. He asked me to call a friend of ours with some information that she would understand. He asked me to call Lucy and tell her something I would never have known. He wanted me to tell her he had seen her and her daughter and husband do something very special for him. I called her and told her he was communicating with me and what was he talking about. She said the three of them had stood in a prayer circle for me. Validation! It took five whole days for me to convince him to step closer to that light. I asked my guide for help and I asked my friend JV (who had already come through) for help.

They described to me in every detail what happened when he crossed into that light and I wrote down every single word. It took hours for them to spell out the celebration that took place on the Other Side and the messages that started coming through were breathtaking and wonderful. And that was only the beginning of the messages and the miracles to come. The biggest miracle was that I had found someone I did not know was lost. I found someone I did not understand that I had the ability to find. It was the most amazing thing I could have ever been a part of. I could translate every word. It was incredible!

I had pushed these things out of my mind for so long and now not only did I have to accept this direct communication but I had just helped a soul cross over. And the energy increased by triple. So did the messages, so did the visits, and then the healings started.

And I had gone to the Expo to get a psychic reading and have a little fun! Imagine!

I was channeling with my right hand and a crystal and writing with my left.

These are His Words...

The messages started coming in stronger and stronger, hundreds and hundreds of words to write down. Mike started telling me how he was literally trapped on this soul plane, what he saw and experienced and why. My utter amazement that this was happening was also comforted by the fact that I emailed Dr. Mallory-Elliott to make sure this really was happening! She explained to me that he had died suddenly in a violent crash and he had rejected going into the light, and it was not an uncommon occurrence for a soul to become lost this way.

His channeled words:

"I heard Judi channeling and communicating. She was using a pendulum and a piece of paper with the alphabet written on it. She got my message. She spelled out my name. I couldn't believe we were able to communicate this way. I told Judi that I thought my soul was damned to hell. I had witnessed someone close to me performing a ceremony from a book. They were mad because I had left too soon and they wanted revenge. Judi told me this wasn't true and that no one had the power to do such a thing to me. I didn't believe her at first."

"She became very insistent that I go to the light. She asked me if I could see it and I said yes, a little bit, far off. She called to our friend JV and asked him to come and help along with her Spirit Guide, Jack. The next thing I knew I could see JV standing there. I said "Look, a friend with a light!" I shook his hand and he started laughing. "What took you so long to get here?" He could not understand why I had been hanging out with ghosts for all this time; he didn't comprehend why in the world I had not come to the light sooner. I explained to him what had traumatized me and he told me the same thing. No one has that kind of power over me. JV told me that Judi had done an awesome thing by saving me. He said that she was able to communicate with us."

"JV said that he'd been trying for years before he crossed over to communicate with the other side without success. He said he heard Judi asking God to help me. He asked that her gifts be made stronger. God blessed Judi and said that her gifts would grow. Her prayers had been heard and JV was asked to meet me at the light. JV said he was an Ascended Master and that Judi had accomplished something wonderful. She had helped save a soul."

Me??? I felt like it had all happened in a blur, in another World way removed from this one, in a timeless existence where everything was wrapped in complete unconditional love and light. I always knew it was there but this was beyond anything I could ever have visualized or imagined to happen.

Here are excerpts from my emails to Dr. Mallory-Elliott:

From: Judi Lynch

Sent: Tuesday, May 02, 2006 3:12 PM
To: Dr. Mallory-Elliott
Subject: Seeking advice

Dear Dr. Mallory-Elliott,

I had the wonderful pleasure of having a short session with you at your booth recently in Nashville (at the New Age Expo). My name is Judi Lynch and my friends Char and Kim had suggested that I try to meet you that day.

My life has changed in a most awesome way since that Saturday when you sat down after our session and told me that I was extremely gifted. I knew about certain abilities I'd always had but I never imagined that they would grow into something like this. I began to meditate every day after that session and since then I have not only connected with my spirit guide but friends and family on the other side as well. I have had an incredible experience about a friend who had not yet crossed over after an accident last year and I need your advice. I want to be able to do automatic writing. It's of the utmost importance that I am able to record what he is telling me about his journey. Can you give me any advice on how to accomplish this?

Thank you so much. I hope to hear from you soon.

Judi Lynch

Her Reply:

Hi, Judi! I remember you well, and I am so glad for your effort at meditation and the many benefits it has brought to you. If the man is telling you about his journey, you can record it as he communicates it to you and transcribe it? I am confused by the phrase "automatic writing," which means dictation from another party in spirit, which still has to be written down. If you are hearing it now, why cannot you write it down? What am I missing here? Please let me know. Endless love, Louise

From: Judi Lynch [mailto:jalynch77@hotmail.com]
Sent: Wednesday, May 03, 2006 7:17 AM
To: Dr. Louise Mallory-Elliott

Subject: RE: Seeking advice

Hi Louise,

It's so nice to hear from you. Yes, I have left out a few facts :-). I'm not hearing him (yet), he is communicating with me through a crystal. He is spelling out all of his messages to me with a piece of paper that I wrote letters on. I can feel him standing next to me, I can feel his energy. He has moved objects and candle flames. I have passed along messages to people for him (that was so wonderful). He wants me to write down his story but at this rate, it could take a really, really long time! When I asked my SG for advice I was told to contact you. Could the answer be that I need to pray and meditate and ask to be able to hear him? Thank you so much for your help!

Much love to you,

Judi

Her Reply:

Honey bunny, if you can feel his standing there, and he can move objects by capitalizing on your energy field, there is no difference in hearing him or seeing him. Just start talking to him, and ASSUME that he is listening, and

KNOW that you will be able to receive his responses. Start with something very simple like questions that can be answered yes or no. "Are you present? Do you wish to communicate? Are you in pain? Are you happy?" Then just wait to see what happens, realizing that sometimes, the answer comes when you are not concentrating and trying;. Or, just start writing and see if you can feel where your style changes from that of your own. But this man is not yet dead? Is he is a coma? Endless love, Louise

From: Judi Lynch [mailto:jalynch77@hotmail.com]
Sent: Wednesday, May 03, 2006 10:12 AM
To: Dr. Louise Mallory-Elliott
Subject: RE: Seeking advice

Louise,

He was killed in a jeep accident in November of 2004. Of course I assumed that he had crossed over already. He came through to me one day while I was asking my SG questions - quite unexpected! He was so happy to know that he was getting through to me, he had been trying to communicate but said no one he had tried to talk to could hear him or feel him until now. He was in complete distress and afraid of where he was and where he was going. He kept telling me he was sorry for things that had happened, and that he was afraid of how he was leaving this world. This all happened over a period of several days. He asked me to give a message to three specific people (which I didn't understand why these three) I called these people and quickly understood why...these three had stood in a prayer circle for him recently and they understood. He went through a lot of emotional pain while he was here but he was a very loved and popular person. He was also very sensitive and judged himself too harshly. I think this is why he was having such a hard time, why he was so scared. And his passing was very, very traumatic.

During one session, I asked him if he could see a light, he said just a little bit. I asked him what else he could see and he said ghosts. I told him all about the light and what was there, I told him everything I knew and believed. I told him God loved him and he didn't belong where he was and he had to go. That people were waiting for him on the other side. He finally told me he was going to the light. I asked my SG to help him, to call on whoever had to be called to help him cross over. I then received the message from my SG that he had gone to the light along with a "thank you" and "you are awesome Judi" He has asked me now to write about his journey and I promised that I would. He says it is one of the things he has to do now. I hope this explains a little more of the situation :-) I have pages of his messages and he is still as silly as ever too!

Thank you Louise for your wonderful advice...I will let you know how things progress

In Love and Light

Judi

Her Reply:

OH! Now I understand! His soul went on to its own plane, but this portion of his personality was struggling. You did the right thing by helping him release himself into the light. Of course, he is still able to communicate from the other side. You already have more than enough to write down! So the only remaining problem is for you to open up not to needing the interface of alphabet letters. Just do it! Orient your mind to his and start writing down whatever comes to you; you will refine the process over time. Or type it at the computer, or record it. You are already receiving; you don't need letters anymore! Endless love, Louise

Channeled Message from Mike

8 MESSAGE FOR MY NEIGHBOR

On the morning of May 6, 2006 I received an important message from a soul that would leave no doubt that I was able to channel messages for other people I had never met or knew much of anything about. I received a visit from a soul who had recently crossed over. Her energy was very strong and insistent these messages get to the person they were intended for.

Jack gave me several names and I wrote them down. These names were the souls who were there to greet this person when they crossed over. Two of those souls had messages to go with the names. I wrote those down as well.

I was told that these messages were for my new neighbor Liz who I had spoken to exactly three times and not for more than ten minutes at one time. The last time was when she called and asked if we would keep an eye on their place because her mother had passed and they had to go out of town to her funeral. All I really knew about Liz and her husband was that they had moved here from Florida, he had family in this area and they were fellow animal lovers.

I took out a piece of my stationary and I wrote down the date and all the names and the messages neatly and put them in an envelope with her name on it. When I dotted the I in her name, I made a big circle. Not something I usually do…

I gathered up every bit of courage I didn't know I had and called her on the phone. I told her I had something to tell her and something to give her. I asked her to meet me out on the front porch. On my way over I cut a white rose from one of our bushes and I met her on her front porch steps. I told her to have her husband come outside so we could have a witness and she called to him to join us. I told her I could communicate with the souls on the other side and I needed her to verify for me what I had written down for her and that she might want to sit down.

She said "I'm okay, I don't have to sit, and I'd like to read it please". I took a deep breath and handed her the rose and the envelope. She opened up the envelope and started reading my note and I knew right away it was true. The tears welled up in her eyes and her hand went up to her mouth and then she read it again and again and again. Then she grabbed me and hugged me so hard I thought she might break a rib.

When she had let go, I said "So, you know who these people are then?" She said "Oh, Yeah, Oh my God. Yes." and then she finally sat down on the concrete and handed the note to her husband and said "You won't believe this, you just won't believe it. It's from my mother." He took the note out of her hand and read it and looked at me and said, "How did you do that?" I said I wasn't entirely sure yet how it all works, but I knew that I was doing it. The messages and the names had all made sense and she also told me that when she was a girl, she always signed her name with a circle above the I.

I walked back home and sat down in silence for about an hour. That really did just happen. I just channeled accurate and detailed messages for my neighbor from her guides and loved ones. It took awhile for me to let it melt into my consciousness.

She walked over a few days later and told me that she kept the note next to her bed in the nightstand and how much it had helped her and then she handed me a beautiful amethyst pendant as a thank you. It was still hard for me to believe the detail of the messages.

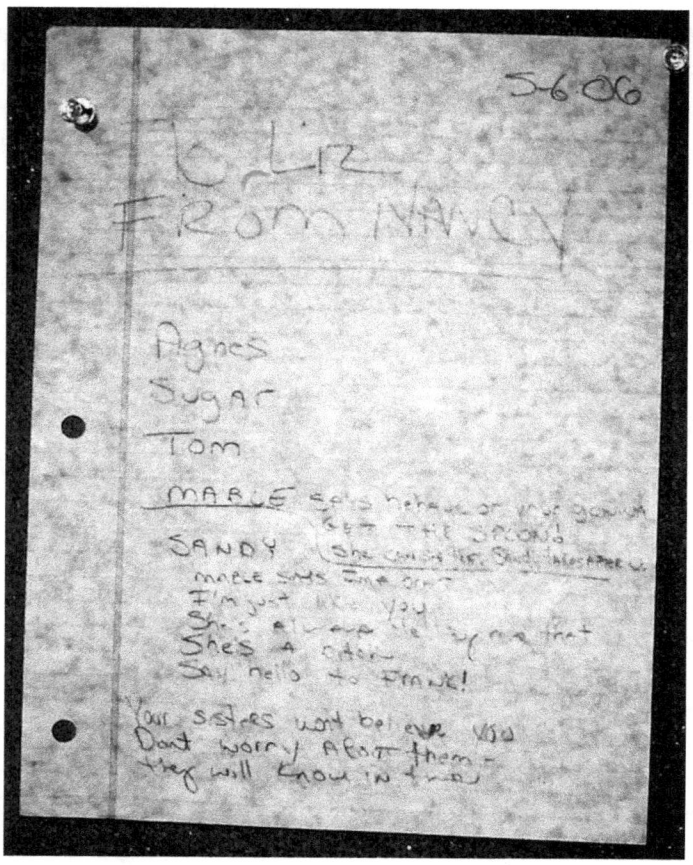

Message from Mom for Liz

9 THE FIRST HEALING

After I composed myself from delivering messages to my neighbor, I sat down at the table to communicate again.

It was explained to me that the damage in my neck was going to be healed through energy channeling. I had to sit very still and completely focus to watch in the crystal what was taking place. They were able to put on quite a spectacular show.

I sat motionless and focused my eyes on the huge chandelier crystal hanging on a large candle holder. I could see JV standing behind my reflection in the crystal and actually see the healing taking place. There was a glow around my neck where the energy was being sent. I could feel the heat and the energy working inside my body at the same time. I was being healed by the most miraculous way anyone could ever imagine and I could actually see it taking place. I have no words to even describe what that was like or how I could ever explain it to someone else. My friends and guides and healers from the other side had found me and I was their first healing miracle.

In the next few weeks, I received many other healings. My back, my sinus and my migraine headaches all received healing. My guides were able to channel energy to hold down my hands and feet so that I could stay still during these procedures and most of the time I could see what they were doing in the crystal. When the session was done, the heat and energy left my hands and I knew I could move again.

During this time, I played music and stayed up during all hours. Candle flames were dancing, light bulbs flickering and projected images were glowing in the crystal. Wonderful beautiful awesome images that would take your breath away when they came into focus. It was remarkable that my guides were channeling images into a chandelier crystal. I also got a lesson in how this energy feels when the souls try to pick up your foot or hold your hand. There was an actual pulse like a heart beating and it started in my hand and went all through my body. My hands levitated off the table and my feet lifted off the floor. It was incredible light and energy, a feeling of joy, complete unconditional love and healing.

One day, they projected Mother Theresa into the crystal and I sat and cried and cried…after that there was a gorgeous church and many visits from several different souls. I was listening to Coldplay, R.E.M., Alana Davis, John Mayer, Paul Simon, meditating, channeling and writing.

10 SOUL MESSAGES AND VISITS

Let the party begin! I started receiving messages and visits and information from everywhere.

Mike was very insistent that I deliver several messages to the friends he had left behind here. Since he was also a friend of mine, I agreed to do that. I knew I had to brace myself for every reaction and try to be ready. It was incredible to me the amount of information and its accuracy. I was not only relaying the information, I was getting validation from several people that it was correct.

Over the next several weeks. I received message after message and visit after visit and I wrote them all down in notebooks and on scraps of paper. Souls I had known in my childhood, people I used to know who had passed on, friends and relatives, guides and healers. The energy projected into the crystal showing me things I could hardly believe as well as actually feeling their presence, their touch, and the healing energy they were channeling.

I started doing energy healings on my family and friends and we documented session after session. I would put my hands on their shoulders, build up the energy field, step back and let the guide energy take over and direct the healing where it was needed most. Amazing! We held meditation sessions with the crystals and candles, asked for healing, messages and protection each time. I had never before even imagined in this life that it was possible to feel and hear and see so many miracles.

I have saved every letter, email, card and even phone message testimony to remind me that yes it really is possible for all these things to happen and keep happening in the future....I wanted everyone to know they had the ability inside of them to heal anything and that the proof was out there. You can really touch another soul with this beautiful light to re-ignite the energy they possess inside and awaken the gifts they have been waiting to remember how to use!

Some early testimonies:

"Judi had become very confident in her psychic energy. I closed my eyes and concentrated on welling up my soul, as I call it. Feeling a glow and energy floating up from my feet and concentrating on the top of the well, a point above my head where the lights flow to. Judi put her hands on my shoulders." "Since then I have not had an asthma attack." Scott L.

"Thank you for the healing energy! My bumps and bruises are healing remarkably fast! In only 5 days it is like nothing happened to me at all. Some of my injuries were pretty bad and should not be healing as fast as they are, so thank you!" Liz F.

In March of 2007 I had my first healing energy workshop. The energy in the room that day was full of light and healing and smiling faces. It was the beginning of many readings, healings and friendships and more shining miracles for us all. It was awesome to feel so much support and understanding. We video taped the whole workshop and I stayed for a couple of extra hours giving readings and healing sessions.

Here are some of the testimonies I received after the Unity Workshop:

"The workshop Saturday was incredible. My friend and I attended and really came away energized. Judi, for this to have been your first was amazing! You were so relaxed and we both saw your beautiful white aura shining so brightly, and at times there were beautiful violet streams shooting out from you. Thank you so much for the wonderful workshop. We look forward to another. " Carolanne

"I just want to say congratulations on a successful first workshop. I attended your work shop today at Unity and I must say it was awesome! I had some second guessing about attending after my mix-up with the time and being concerned about getting there late. But, I am so happy my guides continued to nudge me and I had to return for the workshop. I want to wish you much success as you move forward in your life purpose. I look forward to seeing your success and working with you on helping me discover my purpose as well. Thank you for sharing your experiences. Peace and many Blessings." Ernesta

"You were very on target with me and my friends at Unity today. It was a fun time too. "
Vicki

"I would like you to know it was a pleasure to meet you this past Saturday. You have an extremely wonderful gift and are using it to help others, and we commend you for all of your efforts." Brenda

"I went home so glad and feeling so light after that meeting that I wanted to share with you." "I am so glad to have met you and all those people! I have a feeling that after now my life will change forever." Adriana

"You have such a special gift. I know that these gifts are true and strong and you receive them because of your pure spirit and the desires of your heart. It is a privilege to have been at the workshop..." Dixie

After the workshop, I had appointments for sessions for weeks. Every healing session and reading was one more miracle of light energy. I received notes and letters and emails and phone calls and it made me so happy to know that they could feel and experience this with me. I wanted everyone to know that this was the future of our evolving here. This kind of healing and communication was out there for all of us. We have the capability to heal from so many things we carry around with us, along with healing our souls, which need to be reminded of our true capabilities and purposes here. I knew that all of this was just the beginning of my journey in this part of my life. It was all new to me as a way of life here, but yet it wasn't. It was so familiar to every part of me.

Testimonies from sessions scheduled after the workshop:

"Thank you! I am feeling much better after our session this week. It really helped me to get through. I shared your messages with my brother-in-law and he was amazed. I will keep my sunglasses at hand! Thanks again," Ron

"The best thing that has happened to me in years is you channeling the energy to open my crown chakra! It has made all the difference in the world. My mind is clearer and thoughts don't get stuck in a loop like they used to. My sinuses still hurt off and on but I always think of how my crown chakra is open now and I bring a huge tube of Light in and I start buzzing and relax

instantly.
Thanks again so very much!" Michella

"I am so glad I talked to you. I was looking for clarification and boy was it clear! I am still knocked over by the show of energy. I keep touching my hand just in awe. You are awesome- thanks for understanding, verifying and just being you." Ernesta

"Hello, gee, I didn't realize how much we were in another dimension or light energy until I pulled into Mac's. I feel surreal. Thank you, it was a wonderful session. Here's to white light," Vicki

11 SHARING THE LIGHT

In the fall of 2007, we bought an old country church up on Keel Mtn. and turned it into the Crystal Healing & Spiritual Center along with a non-profit, Crystal Healing Foundation, Inc..

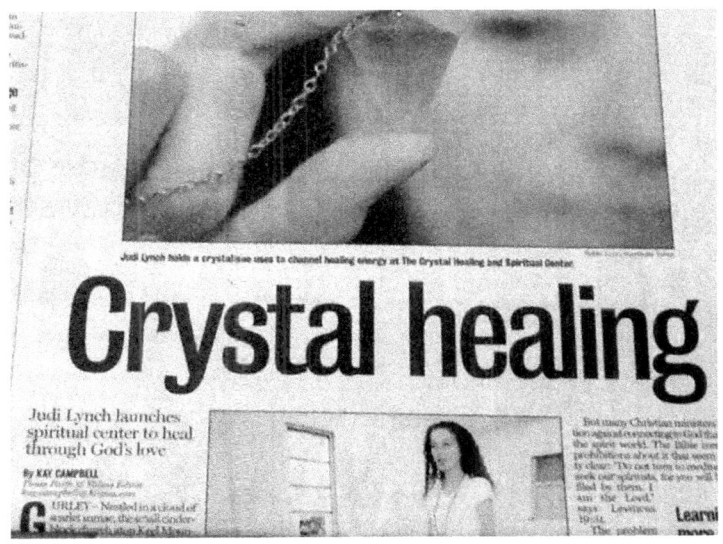

I gave readings and healing sessions, taught classes and hosted workshops on psychic awareness, energy healing and ascension for two years there until my circumstances changed and I had to move. One afternoon after a reading, the crystal I was using to communicate fell out of my hand and I started hearing without it. The energy being channeled through my hand was giving me the letters, words and messages. The person I had just given a reading to was an ordained minister and he had no idea the amazing energy field around him. He had come to ask me several questions about metaphysical and spiritual concepts and to tell me that people were seeing angels at his church. I think an angel must have been holding on to my hand when he left. I didn't need the crystal anymore. Amazing.

The journey continues since that day in the Spring when we discovered something amazing about the power of the light energy that communicates and heals us as we evolve our consciousness. There is a light that shines on us for sure, always was and always will be.....May you always know you have a Friend with a Light.

Endless Blessings, Peace and Healing Light Energy,

Judi

ABOUT THE AUTHOR

Judi Lynch lives in North Alabama and is President of the Crystal Healing Foundation, Inc., a non-profit dedicated to healing mind, body and soul. She works as a Spiritual Advisor, Psychic Medium, Healing Light Energy Channel, and a Featured Columnist for OM Times Magazine online.

Websites: www.judilynch.com

www.crystalhealingspiritualcenter.com

Email:judi@judilynch.com

www.ingramcontent.com/pod-product-compliance
Lightning Source LLC
Chambersburg PA
CBHW061518040426
42450CB00008B/1676